Edexcel GCE History

Coursework Book

Martin Collier   Rosemary Rees

Series editors: Martin Collier   Rosemary Rees

Unit 4 Student Book

A PEARSON COMPANY

Published by Pearson Education Limited, a company incorporated in England and Wales, having its registered office at Edinburgh Gate, Harlow, Essex, CM20 2JE. Registered company number: 872828

www.heinemann.co.uk

Edexcel is a registered trade mark of Edexcel Limited

Text © Pearson Education Limited 2009

First published 2009

12 11 10 09

0 9 8 7 6 5 4 3 2

British Library Cataloguing in Publication Data
A catalogue record for this book is available from the British Library.

ISBN 978 1 84690 509 4

Edited, designed, typeset and produced by
Florence Production Ltd, Stoodleigh, Devon
Original illustrations © Pearson Education Limited 2009
Cover design by Pearson Education Limited
Cover photo/illustration © Corbis/Tim Pannell
Printed in the UK by Henry Ling

Acknowledgements
Every effort has been made to contact copyright holders of material reproduced in this book. Any omissions will be rectified in subsequent printings if notice is given to the publishers.

Websites
The websites used in this book were correct and up to date at the time of publication. It is essential for tutors to preview each website before using it in class so as to ensure that the URL is still accurate, relevant and appropriate. We suggest that tutors bookmark useful websites and consider enabling students to access them through the school/college intranet.

Disclaimer
This Edexcel publication offers high-quality support for the delivery of Edexcel qualifications.

Edexcel endorsement does not mean that this material is essential to achieve any Edexcel qualification, nor does it mean that this is the only suitable material available to support any Edexcel qualification. No endorsed material will be used verbatim in setting any Edexcel examination/assessment and any resource lists produced by Edexcel shall include this and other appropriate texts.

Copies of official specifications for all Edexcel qualifications may be found on the Edexcel website – www.edexcel.com

Contents

Section 6: Writing up Part A and Part B   **68**

Section 7: How will my work be assessed?   **75**

Section 1: Introduction

1 What is history?

> *History is bunk*

The very fact that you are embarking on A-level History and have opened a book that will tell you how to work through Unit 4, means that you probably do not agree with Henry Ford that 'History is bunk'. But did Henry Ford really say that?

> History is more or less bunk. It's tradition. We don't want tradition. We want to live in the present and the only history that is worth a tinker's damn is the history we make today.
>
> (Henry Ford, quoted in the *Chicago Tribune* on 25 May 1916 in an interview with Charles Wheeler)

So Henry Ford didn't simply say that history is bunk. He said it was 'more or less bunk' and then he went on to explain why. This shows how important it is never to accept a soundbite unquestioningly.

Discussion points

Now it is your turn to express an opinion. Here are some points that you might discuss with other people in your class.

- Do you agree with Henry Ford's explanation?

- Is there any point in looking back into the past?

- Is the history we make today all that is important?

- Does the fact that Henry Ford was a 20th-century American industrialist affect whether or not we accept what he says about history?

Now think about what other people have said about history:

> It is the true function of history to represent the events themselves and to leave the observations and conclusions thereupon to every man's judgement.
> (Francis Bacon 1605)

> What are all the records of history but narratives of successive villainies, of treasons and usurpations, massacres and wars?
> (Samuel Johnson 1751)

> No past event has any intrinsic importance. The knowledge of it is valuable only as it leads us to form just calculations with respect to the future.
> (Thomas Babington Macaulay 1840)

> Those who cannot remember the past are condemned to repeat it.
> (Georges Santayana 1905)

> History is the most dangerous substance that the chemistry of the intellect has created. It makes men dream, it intoxicates them, breeds false memories in them, takes up their ancient grievances and turns nations bitter, intolerant and vain.
> (Paul Valéry 1928)

Task

(a) Work in pairs. How far do you agree with these ideas about the nature of history? Rank each opinion on a scale of 1 to 5 (where 1 = strongly disagree and 5 = strongly agree), and say why.

Comments	Ranking				
	1	2	3	4	5
1 It is the true function of history to represent the events themselves and to leave the observations and conclusions thereupon to every man's judgement. (Francis Bacon 1605)					
2 What are all the records of history but narratives of successive villainies, of treasons and usurpations, massacres and wars? (Samuel Johnson 1751)					
3 No past event has any intrinsic importance. The knowledge of it is valuable only as it leads us to form just calculations with respect to the future. (Thomas Babington Macaulay 1840)					
4 Those who cannot remember the past are condemned to repeat it. (Georges Santayana 1905)					
5 History is the most dangerous substance that the chemistry of the intellect has created. It makes men dream, it intoxicates them, breeds false memories in them, takes up their ancient grievances and turns nations bitter, intolerant and vain. (Paul Valéry 1928)					

(b) Now write your own definition of history. Once you have done this you should explain what you think history is to your work partner.

The work of the historian

Let us look more closely at the work of the historian. Both of the following observations were written by practising academic historians.

Source 1

From the inaugural lecture as Regius Professor of Modern History at Cambridge University given by George Trevelyan in October 1927

On the shore where time casts up its stray wreckage, we gather corks and broken planks, whence much indeed may be argued and more guessed; but what the great ship was that has gone down into the deep, that we shall never see.

Source 2

From Simon Schama *Dead Certainties* published in 1991

Historians are left forever chasing shadows, painfully aware of their inability ever to reconstruct a dead world in its completeness, however thorough or revealing their documentation. We are doomed to be forever hailing someone who has just gone around the corner and out of earshot.

Discussion points

- How far do these two 20th-century historians agree with each other?

- How far do you agree with them?

Maybe we would all agree with the poet W. H. Auden when he says 'History is, strictly speaking, the study of questions'.

Definition of history

Points of agreement and disagreement between historians

Points of agreement	Own comments

Points of disagreement	Own comments

2 What is a historical enquiry?

Notes

Both Trevelyan and Schama would agree that historians try to reconstruct the past. They would also both agree that, whatever construct is made, it is necessarily incomplete. And that is the true excitement of history. The discovery of a diary entry, a letter, a skeleton or a horde of coins may destroy utterly a previously held belief about what actually happened on a particular day at a particular event, or to this person's motive or to the fate of those people. For example, how might the discovery of the diary of Richard III alter what we think we know about the fate of the princes in the Tower?

However, there are different sorts of discovery that do not depend upon the unearthing of fresh evidence. These are the discoveries that depend on asking new questions of the evidence we already have about past events and people. These are the questions that ask for evidence for a specific viewpoint, interpretation or judgement, and then go on to challenge that evidence.

You will have studied History in Years 7, 8 and 9, probably at GCSE, and definitely at AS. Throughout, you are likely to have been working through a number of enquiries, such as 'Why was Thomas Becket murdered?', 'The Great Fire of London: accident or arson?', 'Why did the Holocaust happen?' and 'What was Gandhi's contribution to Indian independence?' How many of your enquiries can you remember? What impact did they make on you?

Enquiries undertaken

Name of enquiry	What I did	What I liked about the enquiry	What I disliked about the enquiry

These enquiries are set up by the textbook writer. You are given some information and some sources and you are asked to weigh the evidence in order to reach a balanced conclusion. But consider the excitement involved in asking your own questions, in selecting and challenging the material you yourself have selected and in reaching your own, individual and possibly completely original conclusions based on the evidence you have determined.

Enquiry, then, is at the heart of the historian's quest for an understanding of the historical moment. We can never be absolutely sure why something happened at a particular moment in time but, as historians, we can embark on a process of discovery that will allow us to form our own conclusions and present our own interpretations. Our interpretations may differ; we might, in time, and in the light of new discoveries or on reflection, come to refine or redefine our interpretations, but that is the richness of history. It is our pursuit of enlightenment, of understanding and of enrichment. Above all, historical enquiries must reflect our endeavour to be true to the past and to the people who lived there.

3 What is the point of coursework?

Coursework reflects, in examination terms, the very heart of the historian's task: that of enquiry. In Units 1, 2 and 3 you are examined on your ability to select and deploy appropriate knowledge and, in Units 2 and 3, you also need to factor in source evaluation and link this with your own knowledge.

However, it is coursework alone that enables you to set up your own enquiry, to select appropriate source material and to combine this with your own contextual knowledge to reach a balanced, supported judgement – without the constraints of a timed examination. In other words, it is coursework that enables you to work as a historian would and to show those examining you that you can do this.

Furthermore, your coursework is assessed in a totally different way from the other three units. Your coursework enquiry is marked by your teacher and the awarding body, Edexcel, will simply look at a sample of the marked work from your exam centre to make sure your teacher is marking in line with all the other teachers throughout England and Wales.

Notes

4 What have students said about coursework?

Women are too often hidden from history. My enquiry led me to explore the life of a woman who has been ignored by mainstream history.

Coursework meant that I could explore a problem that really interested me.

The most difficult part of the enquiry was getting the focus of the question right. Once that was done, it was more or less plain sailing.

History is usually written by the victors. Coursework enabled me to explore how the underdogs acted and reacted.

For the first time I felt I was working as a historian and this has inspired me to carry on doing this at university.

I really enjoyed challenging the sources I had found to force them to give up their secrets.

I usually panic during a timed exam. Coursework meant that I could take a much more relaxed attitude to being assessed.

Discussion points

• What do you expect from your coursework enquiry?

• Once you have discussed this within your group, write a brief paragraph outlining your expectations

Section 2: How is Edexcel's coursework structured?

Notes

All the coursework you will need to do for Edexcel is located in Unit 4, which is called 'Historical enquiry'. This gives you a very strong clue about the approach you should use. You will be carrying out an enquiry that will investigate aspects of a chosen theme over a period of at least 100 years.

1 Who chooses the theme?

Your teacher will choose the 100-year period and the theme. This will be linked in some way to the topics you have studied for Units 1–3 so that your whole course has coherence. Edexcel has designed over 45 coursework programmes from which your teacher may select your programme, or your teacher may devise his or her own coursework programme (which will have been approved by Edexcel). Examples of coursework programmes are:

- Islam and the Creation of an Islamic Civilisation c.570–c.750
- Rebellion and Disorder in Tudor England 1485–1587
- India: from Mughal Empire to the British Raj c.1700–c.1857
- The USA: from Reconstruction to Civil Rights c.1877–1981
- The Middle East and the Arab–Israeli conflict c.1900–2001

2 Will I be taught anything?

You're not on your own! Your teacher will teach a short introductory course that will provide you with an overview of the key strands of development in the chosen topic over a period of at least 100 years. It will also provide you with the context within which you can choose and develop your coursework assignment.

As you work through this introductory course, you should be thinking about the areas within which you might like to focus your enquiry. It would probably be helpful if you grouped your initial thinking into three main sections:

- factors that helped bring about change
- individuals involved in the process of change
- key events that marked the process of change.

Coursework programme title _____

Factors	Individuals	Key events

3 How will my enquiry be structured?

You have to write one assignment, which is a single essay, in two parts. There is a maximum of 4,000 words for the two parts, taken together, and you *must not exceed this.*

Part A (Depth enquiry)

For this part, you complete an in-depth enquiry into the short-term significance of a key event, individual or factor within the period you have studied. You explore and evaluate a range of sources that are contemporary to the period, along with relevant secondary sources, in order to assess the immediate impact of your chosen factor, individual or event taken from within the 100-year period.

Part B (Breadth enquiry)

For this part, you set your chosen event, factor or individual within a broader context, and explore the process of change over the whole period. You demonstrate your ability to conduct an enquiry by showing your independent use of a wide range of material and using other data as appropriate. You will *not* be required to evaluate any source material.

To show you how the A and B parts of the assignment might be linked, here are three examples:

1 The 'Golden Age' of Spain, 1474–1598

(A) What, in your view, was the short-term significance of Hernan Cortes, the conqueror of Mexico, in the development of Spanish power?

(B) Assess the significance of the role of individuals in the growth of Spanish power in the years 1474–1598.

2 The Changing Role of Women, c.1850–c.1950

(A) What, in your view, was the short-term significance of the role of the suffragettes at this time?

(B) Assess the significance of popular pressure in bringing about change to the role and status of women in the years 1850–1950.

3 The Making of Modern Russia, 1856–1964

(A) How significant were the effects of the outbreak of war in 1914 on Russian government and politics at the time?

(B) To what extent do you consider that the outbreak of war in 1914 was a key turning point in the development of modern Russia in the years 1856–1964?

It isn't necessary for you to link the A and B parts of the assignment in this way. You could, for example, ask:

4   *Roman Britain, c.43–c.300*
   (A)   What, in your view, was the short-term significance of the building of Watling Street?

   (B)   In considering the process of change in Roman power and control in Britain throughout the whole period, how far can the revolt of the Iceni be seen as the key turning point?

5   *The Changing Nature of Warfare 1845–1991*
   (A)   What, in your view, was the short-term significance of Air Chief Marshall Sir Arthur Harris?

   (B)   Assess the significance of the deployment of new technology in influencing warfare in the years 1845–1991.

4 Who chooses the enquiries?

Edexcel is entirely flexible about this.

- The student may propose both the Part A and Part B enquiries they wish to explore.

- The teacher may set one enquiry and leave the student to propose the second enquiry.

- The teacher may set both the Part A and Part B enquiries, which are different for every student.

- The teacher may set both the Part A and Part B enquiries, which are the same for all students.

The most common approach is that the teacher will teach the overview, set the same Part B enquiry for all students and then students will pursue their own depth enquiries in response to Part A of the assignment. However, whatever combination your teacher selects, it is vitally important that you work closely with him or her. If you are selecting one or both of your enquiries, it is your teacher who will need to approve your proposal.

Notes

Section 3: Preparing for Part B

Notes

1 Part B focus and themes

It may seem strange that we are starting with Part B rather than Part A, but Part B focuses on the overview of the historical period in question. As suggested in Section 2, your teacher will probably set up an overview for your Part B enquiry. The overview introduces the main themes or strands that you will follow in your study of 100 (or more) years of history. The themes or strands covered depend on the chosen coursework programme. Their importance is that they provide a context for your study and help you to understand the course content much better. Your task is to define and explain the main themes of your topic in your own words.

Here are some examples for your consideration. The first example is from the coursework programme 'Representation and Democracy in Britain 1830–1931'. Here are some of the themes that run through and inform this topic:

- conservatism
- reform
- democracy
- pressure from below
- revolution
- impact of war
- impact of education.

Another example can be taken from the topic 'Ireland and the Union 1815–1822'. Here are some of the themes of this topic:

- nationalism
- unionism
- Orangism
- Home Rule
- constitutionalism
- revolutionary violence.

The following pages should be used to record the focus of your coursework programme and the course content, which will be provided by your teacher. You should then write down the main themes of the course and define them.

We have given an example of this (see page 14) using some of the themes that have been identified and explained as part of the study of 'Ireland and the Union 1815–1922'.

The teacher has spent the first few lessons of the unit outlining and explaining these and other themes that run through the course. One of the candidates has written in her notes her explanation of these themes in her own words.

Focus, content, themes: an example

Focus	Ireland and the Union 1815–1922
Course content	• The constitutional relationship between Britain and Ireland in the early 19th century. • The leadership and objectives of the Protestant and Catholic communities in the period. • The response of the British government to pressure for change in Ireland. • Partition of Ireland and reasons for it.
Themes	
Nationalism	Is the belief in the nation state. In the Irish context it is used to describe the idea of an Ireland with its own natural identity distinct from Britain. Although not initially or exclusively so, nationalism becomes identified with the Catholic community in the country.
Unionism	Is the belief in protection of and maintaining the Union of Ireland with Britain. Unionism was popular in both the north and south of Ireland but was especially strong in Ulster, which had a Protestant majority.
Orangism	This is used to describe the mentality of the members of the Orange Order. Created to protect the interests of Ulster Protestants, the Orange Order bitterly opposed the Catholic Church, Catholic culture and Irish nationalism.
Home Rule	Is the idea of some form of self government for Ireland but maintaining some constitutional links to Britain. The issue of Home Rule was to dominate British politics and the relationship between Britain and Ireland between the 1880s and the outbreak of the First World War.
Constitution-alism	This is the belief that the best way to bring about change was to work within the constitution. Those who supported Home Rule were, in the main, constitutionalists.
Revolutionary violence	Those who believed in revolutionary violence argued that the use of force was the most effective way of bringing about change. Some supporters on both unionist and nationalist sides argued at various points in this period that the only way they could protect their interests and bring about change as desired was to threaten or use violence.

Notes

Focus, content, themes

Focus	Course content	Themes

Focus, content, themes

Focus, content, themes

2 Change over time

The main focus for the Part B section of your coursework is on the concept of change. In completing your enquiry, you should track the themes identified in the table above. There are three components to your enquiry. They can be explained by answering the following related questions.

- **The extent of change**: From the start to the end of the period in question, how far have things changed and how far have they stayed the same?

- **Causes of change/continuity**: What factors have caused change? Which individuals have been of significance in the process of change?

- **Turning points**: What are the important turning points? What was the state of affairs before and after the event in question?

When you have completed your enquiry, you should complete the table on the following pages (pages 20–9). Here is an example of how you should fill in the table. The theme is from the coursework programme 'The making of modern Russia, 1856–1964'.

Theme	Agricultural modernisation	
Extent of change	**Causes of change/continuity**	**Turning points**
<u>Changes from 1856 to 1964</u> Collectivisation of agriculture Modernisation of agricultural machinery Scientific farming Increasing state control and central planning <u>Continuity from 1856 to 1964</u> Peasants still tied to the land Inefficiency in agriculture remained	<u>Causes of change</u> Defeat in war Revolution Reforming autocracy Improved machinery State intervention Individuals: e.g. Stolypin, Khrushcher <u>Causes of continuity</u> Lack of investment capital Poor education Rural conservatism	Emancipation of serfs 1861 Stolypin's reforms 1906–1914 Collectivisation 1928–1933 Virgin Lands programme 1954–1964

Theme		
Extent of change	Causes of change/continuity	Turning points

Theme		
Extent of change	**Causes of change/continuity**	**Turning points**

Theme		
Extent of change	Causes of change/continuity	Turning points

Theme		
Extent of change	**Causes of change/continuity**	**Turning points**

Theme		
Extent of change	Causes of change/continuity	Turning points

Theme		
Extent of change	**Causes of change/continuity**	**Turning points**

Theme		
Extent of change	Causes of change/continuity	Turning points

Theme		
Extent of change	**Causes of change/continuity**	**Turning points**

Preparing for Part B

Theme		
Extent of change	Causes of change/continuity	Turning points

Theme		
Extent of change	**Causes of change/continuity**	**Turning points**

Section 4: Preparing for Part A of your enquiry

Notes

The key to a successful enquiry is asking the right enquiry question. The right enquiry question will lead you to explore a range of interesting and relevant sources, evaluate them within the proper historical context and reach a valid, supported judgement that will do well when it is assessed. Remember, too, that Part A focuses on the short-term significance of an event, factor or individual.

1 How short is 'short-term significance'?

'Short-term' could be just the twelve months following a specific event or the time-frame within which you want to look at a particular individual. It must not be longer than 20 per cent of the period being studied. In other words, as you will be looking at a period of approximately 100 years, it should not be longer than 20 years.

2 How can I ask the best Part A enquiry question?

Your enquiry will be an in-depth investigation into the short-term significance of a factor, individual or event you have chosen. Because it's an investigation, you want to be sure you don't simply describe what happened. So your enquiry question must lead you away from the temptation to do this. You need to be sure you evaluate, challenge and weigh the evidence you uncover, and this is what your enquiry question must lead you to do.

Your starting point is to use the types of question 'stems', that will help you to do this. A question stem is really a shorthand way of talking about a question structure. The following are question stems that will form the structure of a successful Part A enquiry:

- How significant was ... ?
- Assess the impact of ...
- How important were the consequences of ... ?
- What was the short-term significance of ... ?
- What was the short-term contribution of ... ?

Go back to the grid you completed on page 11, where you identified various factors, events and individuals concerned with the process of change. Now list them in the left-hand column of the grid opposite. In the middle column jot down, briefly and in note form, how the factor, event or individual contributes to change. In the right-hand column, have a go at writing an enquiry question using the question stems above. The first one has been done for you as an example:

Focus of enquiry: an example

Possible focus of enquiry	Contribution to change	Possible enquiry question
Florence Nightingale	*Nursing at Scutari; possible better administrator than nurse.* *Very controversial at the time. Could have been running a death camp!* *Did conditions in the Crimea improve <u>because</u> of her or <u>in spite</u> of her?*	*What was the short-term significance of Florence Nightingale's time in the Crimea?*

Focus of enquiry

Possible focus of enquiry	Contribution to change	Possible enquiry question

You should by now have three or four possible enquiries, some of which you will find more interesting than others. Which should you choose, and which will work well? Sort out two that most appeal to you.

3 Will this enquiry work?

For each enquiry you are contemplating, complete the checklists on the following pages.

Once you have completed the grids, you will need to select the enquiry that will work for you. Consider the following points:

- Do you have a range of secondary resources you can use to provide the context of your enquiry?

- Have you identified (don't just guess!) some useful contemporary source material that is of direct relevance?

- Does the enquiry itself generate 4 or 5 issues you want to explore?

- Are you interested in pursuing this line of enquiry?

If you can answer with a firm 'yes' to all four questions, then you have the ideal Part A of your assignment.

Go for it!

Notes

Check it out!

Proposed enquiry question: _____

	Yes	No
Does the enquiry fall within my 100-year course of study for Unit 4?		
Does the enquiry question require me to reach a conclusion about the short-term significance of an individual, event or factor?		
Is the enquiry focused on a factor, individual or event important nationally or locally?		
Can I find a range of secondary source material? List 5 resources: 1 _____ 4 _____ 2 _____ 5 _____ 3 _____		
Can I find a range of contemporary source material? List 5 that would be useful for analysis and evaluation: 1 _____ 4 _____ 2 _____ 5 _____ 3 _____		
Can I think of 4 or 5 issues that I will want to address? 1 _____ 4 _____ 2 _____ 5 _____ 3 _____		
Is this enquiry a good choice for Part A of my coursework assignment?		

Check it out!

Proposed enquiry question: _____

	Yes	No
Does the enquiry fall within my 100-year course of study for Unit 4?		
Does the enquiry question require me to reach a conclusion about the short-term significance of an individual, event or factor?		
Is the enquiry focused on a factor, individual or event important nationally or locally?		
Can I find a range of secondary source material? List 5 resources: 1 _____ 4 _____ 2 _____ 5 _____ 3 _____		
Can I find a range of contemporary source material? List 5 that would be useful for analysis and evaluation: 1 _____ 4 _____ 2 _____ 5 _____ 3 _____		
Can I think of 4 or 5 issues that I will want to address? 1 _____ 4 _____ 2 _____ 5 _____ 3 _____		
Is this enquiry a good choice for Part A of my coursework assignment?		

Check it out!

Proposed enquiry question: _____

	Yes	No
Does the enquiry fall within my 100-year course of study for Unit 4?		
Does the enquiry question require me to reach a conclusion about the short-term significance of an individual, event or factor?		
Is the enquiry focused on a factor, individual or event important nationally or locally?		
Can I find a range of secondary source material? List 5 resources: 1 _____ 4 _____ 2 _____ 5 _____ 3 _____		
Can I find a range of contemporary source material? List 5 that would be useful for analysis and evaluation: 1 _____ 4 _____ 2 _____ 5 _____ 3 _____		
Can I think of 4 or 5 issues that I will want to address? 1 _____ 4 _____ 2 _____ 5 _____ 3 _____		
Is this enquiry a good choice for Part A of my coursework assignment?		

Check it out!

Proposed enquiry question: _____

	Yes	No
Does the enquiry fall within my 100-year course of study for Unit 4?		
Does the enquiry question require me to reach a conclusion about the short-term significance of an individual, event or factor?		
Is the enquiry focused on a factor, individual or event important nationally or locally?		
Can I find a range of secondary source material? List 5 resources: 1 _____ 4 _____ 2 _____ 5 _____ 3 _____		
Can I find a range of contemporary source material? List 5 that would be useful for analysis and evaluation: 1 _____ 4 _____ 2 _____ 5 _____ 3 _____		
Can I think of 4 or 5 issues that I will want to address? 1 _____ 4 _____ 2 _____ 5 _____ 3 _____		
Is this enquiry a good choice for Part A of my coursework assignment?		

Check it out!

Proposed enquiry question: _____

	Yes	No
Does the enquiry fall within my 100-year course of study for Unit 4?		
Does the enquiry question require me to reach a conclusion about the short-term significance of an individual, event or factor?		
Is the enquiry focused on a factor, individual or event important nationally or locally?		
Can I find a range of secondary source material? List 5 resources: 1 _____ 4 _____ 2 _____ 5 _____ 3 _____		
Can I find a range of contemporary source material? List 5 that would be useful for analysis and evaluation: 1 _____ 4 _____ 2 _____ 5 _____ 3 _____		
Can I think of 4 or 5 issues that I will want to address? 1 _____ 4 _____ 2 _____ 5 _____ 3 _____		
Is this enquiry a good choice for Part A of my coursework assignment?		

Check it out!

Proposed enquiry question: _____

	Yes	No
Does the enquiry fall within my 100-year course of study for Unit 4?		
Does the enquiry question require me to reach a conclusion about the short-term significance of an individual, event or factor?		
Is the enquiry focused on a factor, individual or event important nationally or locally?		
Can I find a range of secondary source material? List 5 resources: 1 _____ 4 _____ 2 _____ 5 _____ 3 _____		
Can I find a range of contemporary source material? List 5 that would be useful for analysis and evaluation: 1 _____ 4 _____ 2 _____ 5 _____ 3 _____		
Can I think of 4 or 5 issues that I will want to address? 1 _____ 4 _____ 2 _____ 5 _____ 3 _____		
Is this enquiry a good choice for Part A of my coursework assignment?		

Section 5: How shall I prepare for writing up the assignment?

1 How do I start?

As part of undertaking an enquiry, you need to take notes. These notes form a record of the information that you believe will be useful when you're ready to pull your ideas together and write Part A and Part B of the coursework assignment. The aim of this section is to give you advice on how to complete a strong set of notes for the coursework assignment.

Organisation

Before you start taking notes, you need to decide how best to organise yourself. There is not enough room in this booklet for you to use it as a notebook. Therefore, here are some suggestions of what you might use to take notes:

- loose paper (or pad of ruled paper) and a file

- an exercise book

- you might choose to enter your notes straight on to a laptop or computer

- loose cards.

Whichever system you decide suits you, make sure that you have a safe place to keep your notes and that you do not lose them.

Collecting resources

As you have already read in Section 2, you and your teacher will decide on the areas of focus for Part A and Part B of the coursework. When you start your enquiry for both sections, you will have a draft enquiry question and areas of focus to work with.

If you are using a secondary source, you must write down its author, title, publisher and publication date as a title. Here is an example of a book used by a student studying 'The Making of Modern Russia 1856–1964':

Laver, J., The Modernisation of Russia 1856–1985, Heinemann (2002)

If you are using a primary source, you should write down where you have found it, its title and author. Below is an example of primary source information being recorded. The book where this source was found was written by Eric J. Evans with the title *Parliamentary Reform, c.1770–1918* and the source itself is from page 116 of that book. The source originates from the *Daily Mirror* newspaper, 25 May 1914:

The Daily Mirror, 25 May 1914, published in Evans, E.J., Parliamentary

Notes

2 How should I find the sources I need?

You should be looking for a minimum of five sources that are contemporary with the period, person or event you are studying and three to five secondary sources that were written later but on the subject of your enquiry.

It would be sensible to start with the book that first interested you in the subject for your depth enquiry.

- Look for a bibliography. This will list the sources the author used when writing the book. The sources will probably be divided into two sections: contemporary and secondary. If not, you will have to trawl through the list and sort out which are which.
  - Contemporary sources will be those written at the time of your enquiry, but not always or necessarily by the people directly involved.
  - Secondary sources are those that are written afterwards and may be giving a particular interpretation.

  Make a list of the ones that seem to you likely to be useful, but make the list under the headings of 'Contemporary' and 'Secondary'.

- Look for footnotes. If there are any, they may refer to other sources. Again, make a note of them.

- You may find, in the body of the text, quotations that seem to you interesting and relevant to your enquiry. The author should have noted where these came from, and you will need to note them, too.

By now, you should have quite a collection of source material to explore for relevance. There are other places you will find source material.

- Collections of documents and other source material. These are published for broad topics, like 'Victorian England' where you might find two or three that are relevant, and narrow topics like 'Well-dressing in Derbyshire', that will be very detailed and might not give you the breadth you need, but you might just find a gem.

- The Internet. If you type the topic of your enquiry into a search engine such as Google, you will probably come up with an amazing number of hits. Be selective!

By now, you should have a good list of contemporary and secondary sources from which to select those that are relevant to your enquiry and useful for you to use because they open up different areas you will want to investigate.

Once you have recorded the source's attribution (author, title, publisher, date) in your notes and in the Book Record table (see below, pages 44–7) you are ready to begin using the source.

Notes

3 How should I use books?

Historians are usually tempted to read books from cover to cover, and sometimes it can be very useful to start your enquiry by reading a general book about your topic, choosing one that tells you what happens.

However, not every historian has the time to read all the relevant books from cover to cover. You will probably find that you are one of those historians without as much time as you would like for reading. If this is the case, you should behave more like a 'history detective', searching through the books to find the information you need.

Before you start either part of your coursework assignment you need to have identified key themes, individuals, events or factors on which you will be focusing. Choose one of these and then go searching for information.

Here is an example in which a student is following the historical enquiry 'The Making of Modern Italy c.1800–c.1900'. They are looking for information about the Italian nationalist Giuseppe Mazzini as part of their research for the Part B assignment. They have luckily got hold of an excellent book, *The Italian Risorgimento* by Martin Clark.

By using the contents page, the student can find the section of the book likely to be most relevant straight away. Look at the contents page (shown on page 42) and decide which pages of the book he or she will read first.

You will probably agree with their choice of pages 37–40 which will hold plenty of information about Mazzini. However, the student should also use the index, because Mazzini will probably be mentioned elsewhere in the book, often in the context of other people and important factors. Have a look at the following index pages from Martin Clark's book (shown on page 43) and find the references to Mazzini.

Some of these page references will lead to pages with plenty of information about Mazzini, whereas others will lead to pages that will have only a fleeting reference. One tip is that you should start with page references with more than one page, in this example pages 56–8 or 68–9.

It is very important that you keep a record of all the books you use. It is also very useful indeed for you to give your thoughts on that book. Use the following pages to keep your record. Here is an example of how you might complete your record.

Author, title, publisher (date of publication), ISBN	Comments	Teacher comments and initials (if appropriate)
Martin Clark, The Italian Risorgimento, Longman (1998), 978 058200353 8	This was a very useful book. There was plenty of information about the role of Mazzini and other leading individuals including Cavour. The book contains useful primary sources as well as a very clear text. I have been able to make good notes on how Italian nationalism changed over time.	

Notes

Contents

Example of a contents page

Notes

Example of index pages

Book record

Author, title, publisher (date of publication), ISBN	Comments	Teacher comments and initials (if appropriate)

Book record

Author, title, publisher (date of publication), ISBN	Comments	Teacher comments and initials (if appropriate)

Book record

Author, title, publisher (date of publication), ISBN	Comments	Teacher comments and initials (if appropriate)

Book record

Author, title, publisher (date of publication), ISBN	Comments	Teacher comments and initials (if appropriate)

4 How should I use articles?

Articles can be very useful indeed in focusing on a specific aspect of a historical topic.
You might also be able to locate articles that explain change over time that could be
useful for Part B of your coursework. There are several magazines and journals that
publish articles at a level suitable for you to use. These include:

- *History Today*
- *History Review*
- *New Perspective*
- *BBC History*.

Your school's History Department or library might have back copies of these magazines.
Alternatively, your school might subscribe to the *History Today* and *History Review* archive
(found on HL 001). You can find out more about the BBC History magazine on HL 002.

You should make notes from articles in the same way that you make notes from books.
You should also record the articles that you have read using the table on pages 49–50.
Here is an example of how you would fill in your record of articles read.

Author, article title, magazine (date of publication)	Comments	Teacher comments and initials (if appropriate)
Robert Pearce, Giuseppe Mazzini, *History Review*, March 2007	This is a very clear article, which explores Mazzini's role in the Italian Risorgimento. It considers the views of other historians and presents a fresh approach, arguing that Mazzini had a much greater impact on the course of Italian unification.	

Article record

Author, article title, magazine (date of publication)	Comments	Teacher comments and initials (if appropriate)

Article record

Author, article title, magazine (date of publication)	Comments	Teacher comments and initials (if appropriate)

5 How should I use the World Wide Web?

The Web is a very useful research tool. Anyone in the world can add information and sources that a historian might find useful. The downside of using the Web is that the information posted often has not been edited and the quality can vary. So, if you want to use the Internet for your research, you must question the accuracy of everything that you read. A word of warning, Wikipedia can be useful but anyone can contribute to it *and change the entries*. If you refer to Wikipedia, treat what it says with real caution.

So, it is back to you acting like a detective once more. You need to be suspicious of everything on the Internet. Before you can trust the information, you need to ask a series of questions.

a) Why is the page on the Web?
The first question which you might ask is why has this page been placed on the Web? Is the aim of the page to explain or persuade, to attack or to inform?

b) What is the website's address?
You should look at the address to see if the website has been published by an official organisation. If it has, the address might be a good indication: for example, .gov indicates a government website, .edu indicates an educational organisation and .org a non-profit making organisation. If the website has been published by an individual, it will often include someone's name in the website address, e.g. 'jsmith' or the word 'members' or 'users'. It is not necessarily a good thing that a website has been produced by an organisation but there is usually more editorial control than when pages have been produced by individuals.

c) Who is the author?
This question should be asked about every source of evidence. Is the author's name on the webpage? If there is no author mentioned, try to find evidence of a publisher. You should be very wary of information published without some attribution.

You should also look for an indication of the author's status. Remember, anyone can 'publish' their work on the Web, so you should try to find out if the author is qualified to write about the subject. For example, are they an academic working at a university? You should also ask whether they are in a position to know what they are writing about.

d) When was the webpage produced?
When was the information produced and has the webpage been updated? If there is no evidence about when the information was posted, you should be very wary of using it

Notes

e) What is the tone?

You can tell a lot from the tone of the writing. Is the author measured in what he or she is saying or is the writing clearly exaggerated in one way or another? Is the author using satire or irony?

f) What are the links?

A good historian will provide evidence of where they got their information from (just as you will when you write up your coursework). This will be in the form of footnotes, bibliographies or clearly identified links to other sources. If such links exist, test them out to see whether they link successfully to the other websites and cast your eye over these further sources to check that they are measured in their tone. Work with proper links should be more reliable as evidence for you to use.

You should use the following pages (pages 53–5) to write down the webpages you have investigated and evaluate their reliability. Here is an example:

Website address	Evaluation of website
HL 003	I read an article on 'The Troubles 1963–85'. The article was balanced with good information and points of analysis. The webpage was dated and recent. The BBC is known to be a reliable source of information. There were excellent links provided which were fully functioning.

Notes

Website record and evaluation

Website address	Evaluation of website

How shall I prepare for writing up the assignment?

Website record and evaluation

Website address	Evaluation of website

Website record and evaluation

Website address	Evaluation of website

g) **What am I looking for in my reading?**

From your reading, you are looking for three main things to help you with your enquiry.

Factual information

In your coursework, you are going to need to back your ideas up. Here are some of the types of information you might write down:

• dates

• events

• statistics.

Ideas

You will be looking for points of analysis to use and perhaps develop. In finding out whether the author has written in an analytical fashion you might ask:

• Has the author simply described what happened?

• Or have they tried to explain or analyse events?

Finally, you might ask how appropriate and useful their analysis is for you. To answer these questions, read through a paragraph or section of the book and then sum up the main points in your own words. You will then find it easier to assess whether their work will be useful.

Quotes

It is very useful to be able to quote from a source in your coursework. You should make sure that the quote you use is from a reliable source, e.g. a history book or an important or relevant speech. Quotes should be short and to the point. They should be used as supporting evidence, so you do not want them to be particularly lengthy. Historians are honest people and, when using a quote, they always write down in their notes the attribution of the quote (including, if it comes from a book, the page number).

Writing things down: You should always write quotes down in full. However, it is not practical to write out your notes in longhand. There are a number of recognised shorthand symbols that you might consider using:

→	leads to	↓	increase
∴	therefore	>	greater than
∵	because	<	less than

You might also shorten words in such a way that you write less but you still understand your notes. Here are some examples:

> gov = government   parl = parliament

It is often easier for you to devise your own shorthand to use.

It is very important to ensure that your notes are clear and well structured. You should use sub-headings and break your notes down into bullets or sub-headings.

As an example, here is an extract from A.J. Armstrong *France 1500–1715*, Heinemann (2003), followed by an extract from the notes of a candidate who has chosen to complete her Part A assignment on Louis XIV.

Protestantism

One of the main charges brought against Louis XIV was his decision to destroy French Protestantism by revoking the Edict of Nantes (1598). Louis was determined to invoke the principle enshrined in the Religious Peace of Ausgburg in 1555, namely *cuius regio eius religio*. One can see why Louis wanted the Huguenots to conform; as the Most Christian King it was his duty to stamp out heresy and promote the glory of his rule through Catholicism. Yet the Huguenots had proved extremely loyal to the crown, even during the Fronde, and they were an important part of the industrial growth that France was experiencing. The timing of Louis' persecution of the Huguenots lay in the personal life of the king and France's standing within Europe.

Notes

Prot.

1. LXIV destroy Prot — cuius regio eius religio.

2. Hugs. Loyal and imp in Ind.

Quote: Timing of Hug. 'lay in the personal life of the king and France's standing within Europe'.

Notes

6 Who else might I ask?

Enquiries can also focus on more recent history. This can present opportunities to interview people who have had personal experiences relating to the focus of enquiry. If you are studying 'The Changing Nature of Warfare, c. 1845–1991', you might find war veterans living nearby who would be prepared to be interviewed. (War veterans can be contacted through a local branch of the Royal British Legion.)

A local enquiry

- Many cities, towns and villages have History Societies. You can use your local library or the Web to get in touch with the local History Society who might be able to put you in touch with someone who can answer your questions. This person might also be able to point you in the direction of primary and/or secondary resources.

- Information about how you can contact local branches of the Historical Association can be found at HL 004.

Interviewing people

Interviewing people has its positive and negative sides.

- The positive side to such evidence is that it gives personal insight which can be used to illustrate more general points being made.

- Care is needed to ensure that the evidence given is not exaggerated or too selective.

Here are some tips to help you if you are lucky enough to be able to get advice or interview someone:

- Draw up a list of questions beforehand and send them to the person being interviewed in advance.

- Take a list of supplementary questions with you to the interview.

- If possible, record your interview so you can then type up or write out a full transcript of what was said.

A word of advice

You might think that it is a good idea to contact university historians by email for advice. Although some university historians might be happy to help, they are very busy people and they might not appreciate hundreds of such emails. If you have any personal contacts who you think would be of use in advancing your enquiry you should use them, but avoid speculative emails.

Remember, all contacts and/or interviews made must be recorded and included in your appendix (see below, pages 65–7). You should use the table on the following pages (pages 60–1) as a summary record for all your interviews and contacts.

Here is an example of how you should fill in the table.

Contact/interviewee	Summary
Own grandfather	His father fought in Bomber Command during orld War II. He gave me a collection of letters and a diary for me to use.
Mr Johnson, Cambridgeshire Historical Association	He was able to give me information about the history of RAF Molesworth including the introduction of Cruise missiles in the 1980s.

Notes

Contacts and interviews record

Contact/interviewee	Summary

Contacts and interviews record

Contact/interviewee	Summary

7 What is a bibliography?

You should attach a bibliography to your coursework. A bibliography is a list of the works you have used. It is listed by author surname in alphabetical order. It will include the following sections of resources used:

- books

- articles

- newspapers

- websites

- films/videos

- non-published correspondence

- details of assistance received from persons consulted: their names, positions and details of assistance sought and obtained

- if no such assistance was obtained you should state: No further assistance was received in the process of this enquiry.

The books and articles should be numbered for easy reference.

On the following pages, there is space for you to write out your draft bibliography using the information already recorded earlier in this booklet. The following example gives extracts from a draft bibliography prepared by a student completing coursework on 'Challenge and rebellion in Tudor and Stuart England 1509–1660'.

Number	Attribution
1	Anderson, Angela and Imperato, Tony – _An Introduction to Tudor England, 1485–1603_, Hodder & Stoughton (2001)
2	Anderson, Angela – _An Introduction to Stuart Britain, 1603–1714_, Hodder & Stoughton (1999)
3	Culpin, Chris; Evans, Eric; Coward, Barry – _Stuart England 1603–1714: The Foundation of the British State_, Longman (1997)
4	Lockyer, Roger and O'Sullivan, Dan – _Tudor Britain, 1485–1603_, Addison Wesley Longman, Longman Advanced History (1997)
5	Lotherington, John (ed.) – _The Tudor Years_, Hodder & Stoughton (1994)

Notes

Draft bibliography

Number	Attribution
1	
2	
3	
4	
5	
6	

Draft bibliography

Number	Attribution
1	
2	
3	
4	
5	
6	

8 How do I use footnotes?

Footnotes can be used to identify an attribution or a source. However, footnotes should *not* be used to provide more information, or to develop points and arguments made in the text; and they should not contribute directly to the analysis or explanation. The following list describes how to use footnotes and also gives examples.

- A historian's views, when cited in your assignment, must be attributed. If the historian's work is not mentioned in the bibliography then it should be fully attributed. Below is an example of how to do this.[1] This is also an example of how you should mention the text in the bibliography.

- If the historian is mentioned in your bibliography then all you have to do is mention the author and the date of the text. Below is an example.[2]

- If you quote directly from a source mentioned in the bibliography you should cite name, date and page reference of the quote. Below is an example.[3]

- Footnotes may be also used for identification[4] or to identify that supporting information may be found in the appendix.[5]

---

[1] Ross McKibbin, *Classes and Cultures – England 1918–1951* (Oxford University Press, 1998).

[2] McKibbin (1998).

[3] McKibbin (1998), p. 45.

[4] He was the MP for Preston.

[5] See Appendix 2.

---

9 How should I use an appendix?

You should include all explanations, arguments and supporting details in the main body of your Part A or Part B coursework. An appendix (plural appendices) is used by historians who want to include material to validate or back up the points and references made in the main text. Examples of the types of information included in an appendix are:

- A speech that is too lengthy to include in the main body of the text: for example, a candidate following an enquiry about Winston Churchill's leadership in the Second World War might include examples from his wartime speeches.

- A map to illustrate where certain events took place: for example, a candidate researching Napoleon's downfall might include a map of the battlefield at Waterloo.

Notes

- A cartoon (which might have been referred to in the text, but not necessarily): for example, the inclusion of the cartoon 'Canon Fodder' in coursework focusing on the impact of the Versailles Treaty.
- A picture: for example, a contemporary woodcut of the execution of Charles I.

Each piece of information included in the appendix should be numbered. On the next page is an appendix planning sheet. You fill this in throughout the enquiry as and when appropriate. The appendix number should be filled in at the end once Part A and Part B have been completed. This puts the appendices in sequence as they appear in Part A and Part B. They are then typed up or written out and submitted with the assignment.

Here is an example of how you fill in the table.

Appendix planning

Appendix number	Content
1	Map of the battle of Naseby
2	Charles I's death warrant signed in 1649

Conclusion

You will need to keep all the information in this section for when you complete writing up Part A and Part B of your coursework. The more information you include in these tables, the better prepared you will be to complete your coursework with all the support information. If you have any problems or questions, do not hesitate to ask for advice from your teacher.

Notes

Appendix planning

Appendix number	Content

Section 6: Writing up Part A and Part B

You are now ready to write.

- You might be advised to write your response to Part B first before you undertake your enquiry for Part A.
- On the other hand, you might be advised to complete your enquiry into both Parts A and B before you write them up.
- You may handwrite your assignments or use a word processor. Either is acceptable to Edexcel, but if you have ready access to a word processor, it will be much easier and much more flexible for you to use your IT skills to produce your assignment.
- Remember that you will not be writing to time (unlike in an exam), but you are writing to a specific word limit. The overall word limit for both parts of the assignment taken together is 4,000 words. You should aim to write about 2,000 words for each part. There are severe penalties for exceeding 4,000 words, so make sure you keep within the limit.

1 First you *must* plan

The reason why the word 'must' is italicised in the sub-heading is that some students ignore the advice to plan their work and the quality of their work suffers accordingly.

A properly thought through plan is the key to success. In completing the plan, you can think through your ideas fully and prepare yourself for completion of the assignment. In the plan, you directly answer the enquiry question, using the words in the question. The purpose of the plan is for you to work out in your mind the argument in response to the enquiry question.

- The plan should take the form of a number of lines/strands of your argument (perhaps three or four).
- It is critical that the lines of argument in your plan refer to or cover all of the main issues that the enquiry question covers.
- You should highlight very briefly what you are going to put in each paragraph as a list of key sections and key points. The number of paragraphs used is up to you. Some people like to write longer paragraphs, others prefer to write paragraphs that are shorter and more to the point.

The importance of the plan cannot be stressed enough. It is a very important factor in your success. On the following two pages are planning grids for you to use when planning your Part A and Part B assignments. Below is an example showing you how to fill in the grids on pages 70 and 71. The enquiry question has been taken from the coursework programme 'The Making of Modern Italy, c.1800–1900'.

How significant was foreign influence in shaping Italian political development in the years 1800 to 1990?

Plan for Part B: Example

Points of argument	• Foreign influence was highly significant in that it both hindered and promoted political unity • Foreign ideas from liberalism and nationalism, which were the legacy of Napoleonic Rule, to socialism were to have a profound influence • Diplomacy and military intervention were important in shaping the course of Italian unification • However, the significance of foreign influence should not be exaggerated, Italian political development was very much shaped by internal factors including Church, the Risorgimento and a unique political culture.
Paragraph 1	Foreign influence leading to change; France, Britain, Prussia
Paragraph 2	Extent of change promoted by foreign ideas
Paragraph 3	Foreign influence as a brake on political development
Paragraph 4	Foreign influence, the Church and change
Paragraph 5	Weigh up foreign against internal factors

Notes

Plan for Part A

Points of argument	• _____ • _____ • _____ • _____ • _____ • _____ • _____
Paragraph 1	
Paragraph 2	
Paragraph 3	
Paragraph 4	
Paragraph 5	

Plan for Part B

Points of argument	• _____ • _____ • _____ • _____ • _____ • _____ • _____
Paragraph 1	
Paragraph 2	
Paragraph 3	
Paragraph 4	
Paragraph 5	

2 Structure your paragraphs

Notes

Marks are easily thrown away because your essay technique is not as strong as it should be. The aim of this section is to give you guidance on how to write an assignment that is analytical throughout.

Introduction

Once you have written a plan you need to write an introduction that answers the enquiry question and defines the key terms.

- The introduction will involve writing out the main points from the plan.
- It is essential that you address the enquiry question directly in the introduction.
- Your introduction should be straightforward, direct and deliver an answer to the enquiry question.

Paragraph structure

You need to structure your assignment into clear and well-structured paragraphs. To achieve the mark you want, you need to stay focused on the argument throughout. This means that you explicitly answer the enquiry question throughout the essay. The best structure for every paragraph is thus:

- **Argue** At the start of the paragraph, you should present a line of argument. The best way to do this is to use the language of argument:
  - One should argue that…
  - It is clear that…
  - Fundamentally…
  - Without doubt…
  - Moreover…

  Try to avoid a descriptive start because this will often lead to a descriptive paragraph.

- **Explain** The next section of each paragraph will explain that line of argument.

- **Give evidence** For example, 'The clearest example of this point is the…' This section of the paragraph should give and explain the relevance of detail that you are using to back up your argument. This detail needs to be accurate, well selected and relevant. What is meant by detail? Facts, statistics, names, events, references to historians. *Remember*, in the Part A enquiry question, you are going to need to refer to and evaluate the primary sources used.

72

- **Reiterate**. The last sentence of the paragraph should be a reiteration, going back to the main theme/argument in the enquiry question.

The next paragraph: It is good technique sometimes to explicitly link the paragraphs together. You should try to avoid using the same prefix to open every paragraph as it can become too repetitive.

Conclusion

Your conclusion should summarise the main points of analysis in your assignment.

Here are two extracts from Part B and Part A assignments where the candidates have attempted to work towards the advised structure.

Example A

This is an extract from a Part B assignment answering the enquiry question:

'How effectively did the rulers of Italy advance the cause of national unity in the period 1800 to 1900?'

> However, to say that the rulers of Italy did not further the cause of national unity solely through choice would be inaccurate. Italy also harboured several institutional obstacles to national unity. At the heart of these is the, almost consistently rocky, relationship shared between the Church and state. Italy could never truly be unified if such a chasm remained. Almost throughout the period the Church stood in direct competition with the state. Giolitti, in 1904, described the Church and state as 'two parallel lines, which should never meet'.[1] This is clear at the beginning of the period, as the Church had temporal power and the backing of Austria and the Church opposition to the state was strong. In 1843, the Primato claimed the pope should lead a federal Italy. But, this would have meant going against the Austrians for the cause of Italy. Pius the IX was not prepared to do so and the allocution followed. This attitude was strengthened by the 'Syllabus of Errors' in 1864, again put forward by Pius IX. However, the state was as guilty as the Church in terms of fuelling the quarrels. The anti-clerical law of the 1860s and '70s showed this. But there were also smaller compromises reached. For example in 1871, a compromise was reached through the Laws of Guarantees. Yet, although these helped to improve the state–Church relationship, they did not signify a promotion of the cause of national unity.
>
> [1]   Clark, Martin, *Modern Italy 1871–1995*, Longman (1996) page 146.

Notes

Example B

The candidate has completed an enquiry on the impact of the Anti-Corn Law League as part of the coursework programme 'Challenging Authority: from Corresponding Societies to the Poll Tax, 1789–1992'. She is answering the enquiry question:

'To what extent were the efforts of the Anti-Corn Law League insignificant in the abolition of the Corn Laws?

One should consider that the message of the Anti-Corn Law League was more adhered to outside of Parliament. It used popular propaganda in order to spread antipathy towards the Corn Laws; in 1840, Cobden claimed: 'It is better to use the word "bread tax" than Corn Law; "bread tax" is a good term to fix upon our opponents.'[1] The campaigning techniques that it employed were modern and significant, varying from petitions and strikes to mass meetings, and the propagandistic apparatus included the platform, pamphlets, the Penny Post, the telegraph and the railways in order to tap into the daily life of the targeted prospective members. Furthermore, the Anti-Corn Law League used the Press, such as The Manchester Guardian, as a vehicle through which they could publicise their message. The official organ of the Anti-Corn Law League, The Anti-Bread Tax Circular, stated in 1841: 'those who upheld the Corn Laws were virtually the murderers of their fellow creatures'. Of course, such a source needs to be treated with great caution given the propaganda of the League but this is an excellent example of such propaganda. Although Anti-Corn Law League propaganda was prone to exaggeration, in 1840 the respected and relatively objective Report of the Select Committee on Import Duties, with Villiers and Thornely, gave a strong objective reinforcement of the Anti-Corn Law League's arguments, proposing that food prices were artificially high. Therefore, the Anti-Corn Law League had a clearly defined singularity of objective and persistence in the face of strong opposition. However, the appeal of the Anti-Corn Law League was more on a social rather than a political level.

[1] Quoted in Norman Gash, *Sir Robert Peel, The Life of Sir Robert Peel after 1830*, Longman (1973) p. 110.

Conclusion

You are now ready to write up the results of your enquiry.

Good luck!

Notes

Section 7: How will my work be assessed?

Your teacher will mark your assignment. If there is more than one set in your school or college, teachers working with the other sets will mark your work as well and come to an agreement as to what the correct mark should be. This is to make sure that the same standard is being applied to the work of all the students.

1 What are the abilities and skills your teacher will be looking for?

In **Part A**, your teacher will be looking for:

- your ability to analyse and evaluate short-term significance
  (Assessment Objective 1: 13 marks);

- your ability to analyse, evaluate and use contemporary source material
  (Assessment Objective 2b: 12 marks).

In **Part B**, your teacher will be looking for:

- your ability to analyse the process of change over the whole period
  (Assessment Objective 1: 25 marks)

2 How will the 50 available marks be allocated?

Each part of your enquiry will have a maximum of 25 marks available. It would therefore make sense to spend the same amount of time on each part and, with a word count capped at 4,000, to allocate 2,000 words to each part.

Edexcel publishes the mark scheme and you'll find it on their website at HL 005. It consists of a number of skill levels and an appropriate score for each. It would be sensible to check out your note-taking focus and general approach against these levels as you work on your research, to make sure that your write-up hits the highest levels possible for you.

3 Can I resit my coursework?

Yes, you can! But don't dwell on that now. It is much better to get the best mark you can first time round. However, if you do need to resit your coursework, you can rework your original enquiries.